T0038499

Tomasz Różycki

To the Letter

TRANSLATED FROM THE POLISH BY
Mira Rosenthal

archipelago books

Library of Congress Cataloging-in-Publication Data
available upon request.

Archipelago Books
232 3rd Street #A111
Brooklyn, NY 11215
www.archipelagobooks.org

Distributed by Penguin Random House
www.penguinrandomhouse.com

Cover Art: Stephen Gill

This work is made possible by the New York State Council on the Arts
with the support of the Office of the Governor and the New York State
Legislature. Funding for the translation of this book was provided by
a grant from the Carl Lesnor Family Foundation.

This publication has been supported by the ©POLAND Translation Program.

This publication was made possible with support from Lannan Foundation,
the National Endowment for the Arts, the Nimick Forbesway Foundation,
and the New York City Department of Cultural Affairs.

Archipelago Books also gratefully acknowledges the support
of the Witter Bynner Foundation for Poetry.

PRINTED IN THE USA

TO THE LETTER

Contents

I. Vacuum Theory

II. THE THIRD PLANET

III. Summer of Music

I. Vacuum Theory

1. Meadow

How did this happen, us going crazy together,
and now we're lying in this trampled grass
that buzzes and hums? Around us the massive
body of the world turns, this era's screams and laughter,

a jet divides the emptiness in squares,
our winged children circle high above,
and with your hand you shift the clouds. It's clear
till Sunday, then a front is coming. How did love

poison us with verdant venom, how did we end up
going crazy together, lying in dense grass, high
on each other—and what's become of time, that hangman
with his tools: chains, digits, numbers?

A pair of stupid fools: one sound, two letters.
It was you I chose, and oh so selflessly they warned
that you will make me lose it. The perfume
of acacias in bloom is my only excuse.

2. WHITE DWARF

Love? Once we let it go, it ran a long way
in our headlights. Tell me, what was it exactly?
Animal? Child? I didn't draw a weapon.
We came to a standstill in the wilderness, looking on

with a thousand eyes, below Orion, a white dwarf
calling to us, and we danced, and of course
I spilled some wine on your dress, not a lot,
but just enough to last until the dawn.

3. Scenario

How I wish you were here. But maybe
the fact is you never were. And that's what created you:
this lack, this shock, this string of loss. There are scenes
on TV, if one's watching a bit inadvertently,

aimed right at you, a transmission in code:
Won't you give us fire? Or: strike me down.
Or: take this slaughtered beast, this sheep, this goat.
For now, we have these winter strolls out by the pens,

in ratty fields behind the school, in the ashen
pelt of nature's womb. You won't survive
alone against the winter, and if given
another thirty-six degrees to revive

the flesh a bit, we'll last until a messenger
comes to our aid with fire. But let's return
to the broadcast: on the scene, Lieutenant Anielewicz
lays out the bodies according to the sequence of events.

4. To Give Water to the Thirsty

Where are you now, what address should I use,
what's your name? Why do you mock me like this?
I quench his thirst then go to wash the glass
in the kitchen for a minute and hear something, a word?

But when I return, it's finished. Were you here?
Did you come with a sponge of vinegar? Who said what?
Why are you taunting me? From time to time we must
brush by each other on the street, at the store,

in the bathroom. Someday. Just around the bend.
You leave the papers in a mess, and you're the one
responsible for all things lost—your own collection
of lost things, is that it? And in the end

will I get to know you, will we meet at last?
Plus and minus, electrostatic discharge in the air,
chatter of sparrows and blackbirds, a flash above the poplar,
dark tracks on the sidewalk, the stench of ash.

5. First Poem for Menelik

Forgive me, but I'm not coming. There's no crisis—
because, according to all the top websites,
some people are so poor the only thing they have
is money, money. What could I possibly give?

It's not the distance—you're a hand's reach away
in that wasteland where you spend your days.
We can even meet atop a mountain poured
from one packet of sugar where you can hold forth.

And time's no hindrance, as you know, considering
our modern means of transport that can carry anyone
quite a long way from here in mere seconds,
even to that other world, without refueling.

What can I bring for you? What is it you need?
Hope? Time, belief in the miracle of oneness?
When the hand, which placed an orange on the table
and then vanished, takes on the texture of love.

6. THE GARDEN

There was no money, but we traveled south
so we could sleep in the grass, eat from the boughs
of a tree that stood behind a stone wall alone
in the garden, watched over by the glowing

sword of the sun. Far off, the sea ignited
and went out like bone burning. Love kept on rising
tall enough for us to hide away in it.
But sometimes in the window opposite

a bearded, crazy composer materialized,
for hours rehearsing fragments he could not
connect. Not much besides: a thistle, biting flies,
a snake run over by the garbage truck.

Sunday a downpour flooded our things, but two
spiders and a scorpion survived inside our shoes.
It seemed we'd given time the slip, but when
you took a bite of apricot, there it was again.

7. Phantom

It's good that you're not here. You'd be surprised
how things have gone. How we have coped despite
the difficult conditions—after all, the river
freezes in winter, in summer runs dry. We're trying

each of the variations on ourselves,
tasting each plant that sprouts up in the yard—
we should be dead already. But this jealousy
is a thorn in the side—despite the fact that you're

not here, we have made progress in the art
of fashioning your phantom, and we're good at it,
though if the power fails, again the animals
come out to howl at the planets. So, all in all,

it's good that you're not here. Your singularity
would grow immense—since each of us still carries
a hollow for you inside our hearts, so we just multiply
and gaze at the sky, at the hole above the high-rise.

8. The Third Millennium

We live in feral times
infernal machines move through our streets
emitting sulfur friction smoke
fire birds fly through the sky
abducting people

we stare at ourselves in magic mirrors
that say you are most beautiful
I know you through and through
I'm with you
I am you

we enter great cathedrals adorned
to resemble paradise
with everything we might desire
dreams an eternity of delights

we enter caves where on the shadowed walls
our nightmares are projected in flickering light
not us but others pretending to die hundreds of times

and in our medicine chests elixirs secret formulas
for old age beauty happiness
love potions tinctures talismans
from shamans priests wise grandmothers

we watch tournaments daredevils stumbling
applause we choose this evening's most amusing

sometimes one of us sets off for the outskirts of town
to do battle with the monster dragon minotaur
in a labyrinth lined with tiles

some never return
others are more successful
they say the treatment worked
yet no one can be sure if one of these nights
a shapeless shadow will caress them once again
and they'll surrender at last to temptation

9. When Do Acacias Bloom?

For Debora Vogel

Who is it that sustains this world? The summer
will be beautiful. We swam in the river
at forest's edge, life packed inside a basket,
such juicy yellow cherries. I don't want to tell it,

but it happened. A father, mother, baby,
the matter of greenery all around: ungainly space
and shape that doesn't want us. I am narrating
the story of a nation that at some point came

to earth and seeded grass, gladioli, nigella,
and gorgeous mayweeds, eyes ablaze. A nation
that then became the earth, and grass grew up,
so many dandelions with their puffs.

How will summer unfold? There's too much space
above the meadow, chimneys, over the empty shop.
Let someone come along, a man or creature,
to blow us all aloft, so we can soar up farther.

10. The Place of "I"

What should I call you? Poisoner? Secret agent?
A flicker that's voiceless, bodiless, yet somehow
communes with me, since when I wake I'm certain
something happened between us, but the bed

is empty, and you close the eyes of those who suffer,
and I find corpses—traces you've been here.
But there you are in that window opposite,
your weapon assembled, watching me sit

in order to glimpse how I write this, letter
by letter. On my tongue I feel your finger.
Will you at last break in? Slap down a period? Zero out
our balance sheet, this tango with duality?

Our hero—masked and only partly seen,
no shiv, no rifle, coming only in a dream,
taking care of his wet affairs, seen all at one time
in a hundred places, but never in the place of "I."

11. The Clock

So many caverns in the body, chambers
abandoned once and for all, darkened corners
grown thick with scar tissue, those rooms
and cellars with the furniture removed,

devoid of any residents. When it explodes,
all matter will collapse. A small black hole
will form to eclipse the cosmic body
suddenly, mid-conversation, creating a vacuum

that siphons off the district's oxygen supply
from under the doorsteps where your friends reside,
sometimes even through the telephone receiver,
stealing the breath from foreign sectors.

Implosion ensues from a difference in pressure between
the world and the skin, from which something's been
removed. Lieutenant Anielewicz, in a vacant spot,
installs the clockwork mechanism of the bomb.

12. Twelve Letters

The fourth night was so hot along the river,
the city stopped breathing, the body wanted
to strip down a bit more, lie naked
at the brink of an era, shocked by love,

electrified. Between us a mass of darkness,
I could care less where your night ends.
Merely the patter of blood, the stubborn fan
with its whirr once again in pursuit, chasing

me thousands of miles away. Somehow you removed
twelve letters from the tiny word *love*, and even so
it kept on living. Running. Those twelve bones
did not last me long. I got some food

two blocks down the way at an all-night shop.
Still nothing stirs the banana palm fronds.
Do you sleep naked? Dream naked? I hope
the messenger's still coming, though he set off hours ago.

13. Pointers

Hey, how's it going there, in that place called *nowhere*?
I've turned on all the lamps in the apartment,
though you can't see the light. It's more a flicker
inside the tunnel just for me—so if I left

through the open window drawn by a black line,
I'd know how to get back here. Your world starts
precisely where mine ends. That's one reason
and also all the reams of paper wet with words.

And the night, quite stifling. I'd like
to have you over for some wine—since then
this routine life would cease, this daily biking
to work at dawn, already worn down from the pen.

But we can only trade places, not ever cross
paths on the journey. And we'll never find
ourselves meeting below the station's clock,
where minutes ever-so-slowly tick by.

14. Heat Wave

Suddenly wind at night. It jerks the net, grabs hold
of wires, of online worlds, of attic lands,
lifting them into the air. Three seconds of cold,
and the body regains three years, three instances.

Wind flares above the power plant, a gust pummels
the window. All the ancient words once uttered
in darkness now derive their answer—one long rumble
of fury, like a muffled curse, and then another,

still more enraged. Most likely, conversations with devils
are much more eloquent, since there's a chance for subtle
sophism and dialog. Between us yesterday
a heatwave nestled on the bed, which was way

too small, so heat kept seeping past the four walls.
Each word retreats back down the throat discreetly,
there's just the body pushing past night's sprawl,
leaving its seal of sex stamped on the sheets.

15. First Crisis of the Reader

Meanwhile, there aren't enough seats
for so many authors who hope
to get noticed by the one and only Reader tonight.
He takes the stage at last, a bit late,
rather tipsy
from the swig of courage backstage.
Applause and flashes, a live broadcast.

When asked, he proclaims
the best of the best, sums up the plot.
Some authors sigh knowingly, some authors sigh
with discontent, and hands shoot up:
But how exactly do you read?
Where, at what time?
On the couch? In bed? At the hotel bar?
Hardback or paperback, kindle or nook?
What makes a book *the* book?

I prefer reading
to feel like a feast. Let it be
a celebration, the Reader decrees.
It's a holiday I get to set, my choice

of dress code, my own ineptitude.
Reading—he smirks—should be done rarely
and reluctantly.
But how do you choose?
the authors want to know. When two storylines
diverge in a yellow wood, is it you—
you who picks the one
less traveled by?
Is that what makes all the difference?

The tour goes on for weeks.
The Reader tries discreetly to wipe away the sweat
from his lip when signing books the authors wrote
themselves. The queue goes round
the bend, writers pushing
their tomes at him.
But he's just one measly person
among the throng of wordsmiths waiting
to be read. Aren't you scared? someone asks.
It's a risky pastime, he admits, let alone
a calling. You should try it sometime,

this occupation of mine, with all its hallmarks
of saintliness. Who knows where it comes from.
I simply can't remember *not* reading
and dreaming in letters.
Then I met a poet. Maybe my sacrifice
isn't so huge. Besides—he quips—
just look at all the money and groupies
to keep me going.

But when it gets really tough,
when an author sends threatening letters
or spray paints quotes from their book
on my door, I have dark thoughts
and am plagued with addictions.
I'm a wreck of a man,
dreaming in fiction, living
in a nightmare.

What a joke—he says, crushing the empty
plastic water bottle.
Can we finish this up?
It's so stuffy in here.
Soon he'll be telling this with a sigh
all over again for the glossies.

16. No Answer

How I wish you were here, had been, will be.
We call this lack a life, and if left free
to grow, it grows toward you, toward nothingness,
since the truth is, your address and death's

somehow converge—out there in what we call
eternity. Where else does wholeness dwell?
Meanwhile, the lack is beginning to show:
nothing to give our guest, we're all flat broke,

as always, till the first. No answer.
Son, they've run out of wine. There's no one here
to talk to, and even if there were, words always fall
short. And then only gestures remain, small

nods. The body, still so shamelessly alone,
can no longer hang on in moderation—
each step betrays too much, each pulse, twitch, jolt,
each premature reply to every question.

17. Ż/Ś

Letters! One of these days, Sergeant Anielewicz
will figure out your settings, box of riddles,
put key to puppet's mouth and open the device.
Long has the soul been yearning for portrayal!

He'll start again from A, a tent out back, on screen
tribes from Alpine peaks out roaming the wilderness
in a blizzard of pixels, baring their teeth
in the snow. A beast will arrive nonetheless,

it's just a matter of time. The Sergeant will find diacritics,
accents and tails that twist this script to a devilish
grimace, a caricature. What is it Ł denies,
what's up with Ą, the private joke of Ć?

And what's all the fuss over Ż's tiny sperm?
Where's Ś escaping to? He has no clue.
Meanwhile love, built by us in the cellar,
makeshift machine of discarded parts, still croons.

18. Lavinia

At last, a fifth wave tips the boat of refugees
into the Mermaid Bay, today so murky,
and the ocean, with its love of children, takes them
on an odyssey, to lay them down in the end

on the sands of Lampedusa, Ithaca, Avalon.
This time, the gods and goddesses keep watch
discreetly on their monitors in split display.
They cheer them on, these Greek and Trojan castaways.

But when one god, from boredom, clicks the channel,
it tips the scales, and then the sea eternal
brings someone back to life on a rocky beach.
Now he sits behind barbed wire, near the freeway,

chewing dry bread and waiting for asylum
to be granted in the land of Latium,
whose daughters of fire-red hair descend,
they say, directly from the horned god Faunus.

19. Vacuum Theory

I wish you were here, I say to the room.
Fall's gone bald, summer has packed up and fled,
its features stiffening as if assuming
a rigid deathbed mask. And everything

here is so sharp, it hurts. Through clouds, the light
slices leaves on the path, slices each lungful,
it cuts this life in two, so that the half outside
trembles in a breath-cloud. No way to tell

the halves apart: it works, this loss economy.
And aren't I losing writing, losing conversation,
word after word, right now? In art, it's easy
to shine—too easy to become state champion.

So, am I less and less while you are more?
Will loss then lose its subject to the object?
If something's gone, you lack what's yours—
when that happens to you, you're no longer god.

20. Mirror

A throw of dice can easily upend one's luck,
just toss them long enough, isn't that right?
Don't you know about such things? Perhaps an epoch
is not quite long enough, nor a single lifetime,

for pattern and order to emerge from numbers.
Better to look from far away. There are isolated
shards of the world still lying here well after
Thursday's explosion, when at last the ancient frame

cracked and the mirror broke into so many fragments
that now the face can't create its arrangement
of lines, its twists of tenderness—a puzzle
of four elements now cut with a fifth, darkness.

And I sat up all night, with the song
of cars outside, and tried to piece together
the dust, flashes, bits into a new reflection,
but time had already dispersed the original's features.

21. Details

This is the story of my confusion: January,
the lamp posts wrapped in fog, spun cotton candy.
Tonight, a thaw has come to this, our glacial land,
and let out all the dead, who now crowd around me

in great number at the kitchen table to pluck out
these maggot letters that are squirming and flecking
the wound. In light, the tablecloth, the paper,
the fading glow of snow, the screen, in it a blizzard—

make up a kind of field where letters go to glory.
Can you read the world? Under snow lies proof
of our cohabitation: I was consumed, was food
for them, these letters that hatched inside me

in a festering wound, in flesh, in mud, silt, waste.
Life, as you know, is but a burning, eating, breaking
down of organic matter into elementary bits,
plus some details irrelevant to chemistry.

22. The Measure of All Things

Lieutenant Anielewicz is on the track
of each unfolding change: first this, then that,
some prints laid down, impressions, evidence.
A beast turned up in Turin, then an orange

on a bridge in Córdoba, two suspect addresses
in Lwów, a third in a dream, fake Ausweise,
a photo with the deceased and DNA
on almost every hotel windowpane,

notebook of names, numbers, charts and keepsakes
still warm from several women, yet they make
but a partial sketch of character. And so, the signs
at last lead Anielewicz to identify

a plot: there's someone wanting to outwit necessity,
the normal course of human life—this lunacy
needs full investigation, a measure of all things
he can apply to man as if he were an insect.

23. A Room

Hello? If you can hear me, give a sign, raise a voice,
strike a tone. I want to know if we have a choice.
Bark in a dream, raise the neighbors, swing a gong,
let glass fly from the windows, let the siren's song

prompt an erection. Let the host go hoarse,
and let the radio shut up, let silence rise
above the street like a mountain peak, like forty floors
of editors accepting slender volumes of moans and gripes.

I'm waiting for a sign. There's time. By now, I'm well
regarded here as a nutcase who babbles nonsense
and sends letters to his own address. I myself
created you, it's clear, but what about the future tense

left for me at some point in a penultimate verse,
from where I took it, where else? Summer is a room,
its window open on the night, and anyone who enters
will see how particles of darkness conjugate.

24. DOG

Stretch of day. Rain. Leaf.
Fur of dog. Hair. Gleam.
Wake and whine. At the door.
Someone comes. A dark form.

Form that holds like a fence
what we mean. It makes sense.
Then a mouse. Flit and squeak.
In his dream, dog takes a leap.

Time keeps score. Rain spits.
If you're gone, then I quit.
Time's an imp. Cheats at cards.
Darkness sniffs around the yard.

Twitch and stir. Fangs flash.
Quickly two or three days pass.
You're not here, a lack that sucks
meat from bone, all my muck.

Then the dusk. Hint. Flash.
Shade of May. Clings to glass.

Shadows mock. My blood seethes.
Won't you come, please free me.

Let me live, breathe the air,
not keep howling at the stars.
Wail and gnaw. Sob. Swear.
Take me far away from here.

Filth and shame. Gas. Fear.
Jaw of night. Grief. Tears.
Sewage sobs through the pipes.
Shift the tone, bring the light.

Fiend that jabs me, prods, pokes,
night that weaves its dank cloak,
twist of shawl, heap of cape,
bind me with a yarn snake.

Weave and twist, twirl the string,
treat me like I'm just a thing.
Then a rat. At the bowl.
Like a king, the tsar of holes.

Twitch and jerk. He knowns pain.
Knows how it drills the brain.
Try to catch him. It might work.
Use a knife, or try a verse.

Knife or verse. Verse or knife.
Rain or shine, you're gone from life.
Flick a whip, or try a lash,
a hundred cities shard and ash.

Death's a fiend. It jabs and pokes.
Jeers at cards. Plays jokes.
Shouts and yells: beat it, scram!
You're a thing, a mass, a sham.

There's no you, just a flaw,
there's no hand, just some fog,
there's no face, just whisp of smoke,
grass not breast, wind not bone.

I am dream inside of dream,
sack of blood burst at the seams.
Thorn in vein you can't get out.
Dust that slips from lip to mouth.

Mind eats up this swarm of ghosts.
Come on out. Scream and moan.
Let me go. Die. Take leave.
Won't you please just let me be.

Lose the key. Rip up the note.
Get it out. What's in your throat.
Then it's dawn. The dog gets up.
Sniffs the bowl. Laps a gulp.

He was sleeping on his bone.
Back all bent, he shakes, groans.
Gives a yip, another one.
The world keeps going on and on.

25. A Few Hours

A few hours—inasmuch as we're just passing through.
Enough to freeze at night in an empty station
or tour around—to make the body move,
battling space and time, to confront

the laws of cosmic gravity. An hour
or two, as long as this day lasts. As I go off
to work and you start in on the paper
and read the news, how much it is you've lost

to investments on planet earth. All told,
a few—if you came in, you'd see numerous
letters running toward the paper's edge, holding
each other's endings right before they jump.

A few—enough for the chair to cool off
and a discreet crew to remove the stains,
erase the indentations, take away the body,
and in its place put sanitized absence.

26. Rain

A glass wall of rain traps us in the bar
and sends red lanterns gyrating, thrilled
by the rush. The yellow dust of Asia
rinsed from rooftops and windowsills twirls

in the gutter in the likeness of forgotten
ancestors and demons who've finally located
a place to materialize. But the incompetent
eye can't recognize a face before it disintegrates

in the downpour. Inside an old phone booth
across the street a woman shelters
with two children, drenched from the deluge,
spray from all sides. A hushed bustle. Gestures.

Chris, dashing for a taxi, hands her his jacket.
We drive away, November, and on the windshield
the smudge of neon, Hong Kong dancing. Perhaps
I haven't told you yet how terribly empty it is.

27. A Photograph

Once again, I can't fall asleep, and so I compose
these words for you—this is becoming our tradition.
You—out there where the future pushes through
like a worm from an apple, only the hole

is in heaven and so enormous we'll all
fall in, along with tenements, convenience stores,
our entire state—let's say it's nowhere—
that's where you are, am I right? And these awful

thoughts lead me on a leash, what I must wager
to sleep with the night, coerce the night to take me
into its gap, its crack, the darkest dark
smeared on the sheets, on a piece of paper

thanks to this organ rising from me now.
Then let your morning light illuminate the night
and let them see at breakfast what remains of time
arranged with pauses, letters, into the shape of sorrow.

28. Wild Strawberries

I'll tell you how it was, what she remembers:
the scent of rhubarb and strawberries in the wild
where she hid and the cries of the murdered,
they do not want to die away. If possible,

please give me pills and show me something simple:
a garden with some beds. I'll keep them weeded
with my fingers and one of those short-handled shovels,
tearing out stalks, arranging them in heaps

with no regret, letting them yellow, turn sun-bleached.
Observing fruit will tutor me in color
and weight, in time. A garden should have plenty
of fruit by which to keep track of the calendar.

And trees that herald the spring to come.
When it arrives, I will be ready. Barefoot, wide-eyed,
I'll lie down in my faded shirt on the earth and hide
under the rhubarb, under the strawberry blossoms.

29. Updraft

Meanwhile, the body, carried out to sea,
drifts for eight days, subjected to the grammar of tides,
this loss geometry. The moon rides high, sometimes
an island comes into view, a display of cavities,
with plumes of pepper and almond trees,
but only the rorqual surfaces alongside
to nod goodbye with the wink of an eye.

30. Poor Painters

Those poor painters, forever going hungry
and moaning about feeling sick, those lunatics
in shirts of paper, rolling loose-leaf with
their fingers stained in yellow, blue and green.

Those poor painters, constantly drunk on credit
and kicked to the curb by the tenement landlord,
those limping down the sandy path in the morning
when mountains come into view, unfolding stands

for canvases in a field of clover and larks. What love
inside the eyes of a model holding motionless at dawn
atop a wobbly chair, inside the body's undulation,
when cats dash out the window and feral sun comes in.

Such cruelty in the drawn out, much too drawn out,
blending of colors. Dying in homeless shelters,
they're only rich after death: museums, contracts
worth millions, eager crowds waiting to be received.

31. Via Giulia

The city's top watchmaker here is the sun,
winding the local clocks and mechanism
of clouds and wind. Also its spinning
dial of streets, fountains, squares, and the thrum

of irksome scooters, the dancing of plastic
seized by the Tiber's carousel. At noon,
the body yearns for its own shadow, refuge
of outline where it may lie down, just as

this city did at middle age. But this time,
the silhouette has hips too narrow, shaky
like flame, the shadow fast so breath can't catch
its shade: body of air, not yet filled with lime.

Life: scraps of paper, numbers, words and cries,
a trace of touch transcribed on skin, a warmth
that's still dispersing, a scent. What went before,
and what it is that's fleeing toward the sky.

32. METAMORPHOSES
To Barbara

How lightly we live! Just beyond the horizon
an old volcano, thought inactive, lets off smoke.
They tell us time's about to burst, same as before,
neighbors are packing, they're closing the roads,

we wake to find signs painted on our doors,
but we keep living lightly. Time so many times
would've caught us but couldn't, we kept changing form.
When time surged forth like lava, we became outlines,

when it blew up, we crawled into the earth,
when it turned trainlike, we became ash cloud,
when it turned sniper, we became but breath,
a feather above the rubble heap, a voice calling out

for the kids to come home. We're the letter excised
from a verdict already passed. The slow dance of flecks
when furniture is moved, the joyful subsiding
of dust as it falls, we are the star of its journey.

33. At the End of the Day

So much light! And I, a man of the North,
go promptly to the center of the square
and soak my skin as in the sea's saltwater.
Rinse out my eyes. So much light, my brother!

Take some of it at least. Fill up the corners
of the room, every inch of basement and
the drawers, then all the way up to the attic.
From time to time, make use of it in winter,

gather your friends around and serve it up.
Lock it in bottles, to be uncorked on
New Year's or a birthday, some sad occasion,
or a wedding, or for nothing at all.

Clean light, without impurities—
not our daily fair. Such light dissolves in coffee
like a lump of sugar, like the sun going down:
not yet, not quite, just wait a second, now.

II. The Third Planet

34. Chaos Theory

From your perspective, things most likely look
to be spinning around the room, the kitchen.
But zoom in, notice the way these steps
arrange a kind of music at the sink

and stove, a rhythm of inherent turns.
Zoom in closer, you'll see the fractals churning
in trails of dust along the shelf, hear chaos' chorus
of coffee spills, wine stains, the refrain

revealing sugar on the floor and what it is
that's dancing, truly dancing. Sequence, order—
the closer you get, the more assorted morsels
look the same. Is this enough infinity

for you? Eternity? On the microscope glass,
a ripped lip of envelope from the trash,
the letter left unread, and shreds of a photograph
slashed down the side, is this enough for you?

35. Effigy

Will summer fail again?—the nightly news
and headlines shout. Of course, our plans as well
will fail along with summer, no new move
to somewhere warm, no changing local

conditions to those in which a stubborn wasp
keeps getting caught in each successive glass
left on a sunny terrace, and at night
the honeycomb slides slowly down the skyline

to fill the empty windows all at once. Such dreams
of leaving shadow's zone will fail, since objects
don't even cast a shadow here and gleam
but for a moment like a spark exhausting

itself with a hiss, a whimper. All of it toppling
down: summer, leaves, civilization. Meanwhile,
this love, this effigy we've flung from the rooftop,
has learned to fly, is tapping at the windowsill.

36. Ghost

So, tell me, what's the difference between you and me?
When I lean right, you lean a bit more to the left.
The world sits in between, and as I'm trekking
through snow to the station, your morning is already

clanging with the rite of Spring. When you're awake
the night drags on for me and, let's be honest, the more
of you, the less of me. The less of you, the sooner I'm cavorting
around town—while you're there, pulling up the blankets

till you almost disappear. In order to be both,
we have to be half, to be not-quite-here,
and only then there's a chance to come together,
two halves, two phantoms meeting. Here, in the scope

of my room, I live this half-life, only half-way
sleeping and don't get up when I get up, half a whole
bottle left for later. And if I've let loose this ghost
among people, let it frolic, let it strain, let it sway.

37. Message

What else can I tell you, what more can I write?
That I perform every act quite cautiously,
cover every trace of us—can you guess
what this means, this silence left inside

the phone for all eternity? Your functionary
will pull our prints from each and every object—
glasses, doorknobs, keys—what kind of evidence
is this, obtained by accosting dead bodies

prone on the floor? And you'll never learn how
to really read such proof. A shadow sways
behind each letter, a place often crowded
with refugees, forever in between, stuck midway.

I've hidden in the details whatever remains:
a screw to some unknown machine left
in a drawer. In vain, Lieutenant Anielewicz
rearranges the bodies, trying to find a message.

38. INHERITANCE

And then when I fell, I felt it, how the ledger
has me down not only for this mass
of roving air and movable structures cast
in winter rays but also for the earth itself,

not only for mobile homes and short-term haunts
ruled by a dynasty of pots and pans, a clan
of bowls, of plates and mugs filled to the brim
with hunger, I felt it, how my inheritance

is also land with surface scant as the area
of a body, fallen, but without end
to how deep it goes—five meters of humus
packed with scorched grasses, orchards, ashes,

books and bone ground down. And then below
this tainted layer, one still working—life smoldering,
still breaking down what did not break down
into range of voice, gas of breath, meat of letters.

39. A Curve

Since you're not here, all this duplicity
is left for me to foster inside myself, doubly
difficult because it has nothing to do
with a person but their lack. Commune

with an absence, woo it, and you'll get the gist,
how it grows as you diminish, how it wolfs down
whatever you serve up, gestures, sounds,
consumes the breath, each word on your list of gifts.

But worst, it holds the fact of its own absence.
Lack of a border between one and zero. Nonexistence
is amid *was* and *will be*, a shadow economy
between what is and what is not nothing,

in short: where are you? Somewhere inside of me
there's a place of least possible energy,
near zero, absolute zero. At night the body
twists toward it in the centrifuge of sheets.

40. Essential Traits

What else can I tell you? You're there, inhabiting
the realm outside the window—the endless
space that grows, expands, and keeps extending,
even now as I write—and you're there in the infinity

of small things that even the microscope can't see.
It's always possible to take the heart and crush it
more finely, break down what seems already dust
into smaller particles the size of galaxies,

it's a matter of magnification. Opposing forces
act on the body in both directions, distraction
and concentration. Maxi and mini.
That's what gives rise to all this moaning and effort

of syntax, style, pronunciation. How to express
this mid-winter instant: sky with clouds drifting
so low they're within reach. And on the list
of prerequisites for life, death is always first.

41. Hair by Hair

What more can I write? From all these crumbs
only my name, if I can but remember
its sound inside your mouth, in basic form,
original, from way back pre-explosion.

Now everything keeps flickering. I strive
to strike a balance between what's revealed
and what conceals the heart. So many particles
of tar are twirling in the air, and only writing

is capable of stitching them to story.
This rule is what they like to call a life:
as long as entropy prevails at sunrise
amid colliding clouds, the winter's war

with time goes on in this illumined kitchen.
The body in a chair defends itself with heat,
depletes the light, the energy, burns bit by bit,
losing hair by hair. But time keeps right on ticking.

42. The Eternal War of Opposites

This all is the fault of the war between us,
this circling, avoiding, colliding, hoping,
this silence, this existence chafed by shadow.
Hence light, hence fire, the world with its flickering luck:

gray meadow at dawn, a burning peat bog
outside Ozimek, a wave of turbid waters
collecting everything, an endless dream
under sheets beneath that window facing the cosmos

until at last the falling snow blots it all out.
But the fire still burns, and you hear the unmistakable
music induced by the rubbing of shadows.
Lure one, and in an instant they'll proliferate

on the wall, a whole swarm. Listen to them scratch,
buzz, groan, complain. They have no language
except for shades of darkness and a blackening,
a wavering in the image, in the likeness of handwriting.

43. Glass Houses

Fall has already come calling in town,
cafés are closing their courtyards, fog at dawn
signals misfortune—the arrival of a new poet,
or a suicide by hanging from a belt above the toilet.

All those who had to leave left long ago,
while those remaining feel regret. Group A
goes on about escaping through the tricky hole
of a bottle's neck. And if they pull off living

inside a house of glass, they just might reach
the sea by river, to be fished out by a shrimp boat
and processed, put on sale. Sadly, though,
the body's not so flexible. Meanwhile, Group B

hangs out with the machine, entrusts it
with secrets and longings, then moves in, inside
its vivid walls, sets up a life, a second life,
a fifth, an eighth. Death will never count them.

44. This Era

I've said goodbye to the twentieth century,
its porches choked with bindweed, its wild weeping
and wild grapevines. When finally the black
patrol car leaves, then you can hear the panting

of the train, the horses snorting, sweat steaming
in icy air. Nervous, you wonder what might be worth
taking for good: a useless notebook, minor
snapshots, cheap religious medals? Forests and cities

along the way sleep like huge dark churches.
I'll not be coming back here, windows draped
with dirty towels, signs of widespread plague.
Below the sand, I've hidden a handful of words

not yet infected. For you. I put the rest outside
along with the still warm body to see how these times
will take care of it at night. What shape this era will carve
in the flesh, what will be left when morning arrives.

45. Clay

When will we begin to read like Westerners?
From mud and boredom, from spit and fear of enemies,
from bones pulled out of sand and stolen quicklime
we've fastened a golem. Nothing's enough for him—

a share of eggs and vodka, a seat in the hen house,
monthly visits from virgins and schoolboys.
He pesters us while cooking, barges into the bedroom,
panting, puffing, grunting, but he can't pronounce

a single word. He's speechless, set in motion
by a complex code of letters, now unknown,
forgotten along with spelling rules in the constant
crisis of education, the shortages and lack

of humanistic subjects. For who can mold
a string of signs so that even a rolled-up paper
gun can open fire, bringing down the ghost
with a round of explosive sound, a flash of meter?

46. Contract

Tell me, do you consent? All your decisions
have been considered, conversations bugged
and letters saved, there's video surveillance,
it's clear as day that you were cognizant.

It's all been bought, there's someone gathering
the proof, the prints you left, skin cells and fluids,
you signed the contract, broke the terms, it's you
who knowingly transgressed, incurred the damage,

you alone responsible. So, they will take
you down a bright glass corridor with cameras
in front of your neighbors—you'll be an example
for children and the rest. They'll place the cage

up high and visible from all directions
so everyone can spit, curse, throw a stone,
feel a shiver, grow oddly heated, then clear the mind
and take a keepsake photo of the fight.

47. Cocoon

Soon snow will cover the town and republic,
wrapping the houses for Christmas like presents
in icing, powder, tissue paper, fluffing our beds
and muffling misguided steps of friends

more or less drunk, of secret agents and the scum
of the earth, all circling in orbit. Cats excluded.
No dogs or crows. Then snow will cocoon us,
feed us Prozac, hush us, ban us from looking

outside, forbid us words and smiles and gestures.
We'll vegetate for a long time and hang in suspense
from the rafters, turning our fatty existence
into a winged form. Before the start of summer,

we'll dig ourselves out of our private muck
of subtext, shed the weight, what once was us,
until at last the mirror smiles at the sight of us,
and we fly off, empty, headed for the nearest lightbulb.

48. Settings

How the old Demon seizes us! And we're reset
in the New Year again. It's a curse from the war:
it scatters us, pulls us apart. A Father there,
a Mother over here, the Neighbor Lady somewhere

about here, a Policeman, a Sister and Brother.
But this spot, empty. Isn't it true this Polish family
once lost a child? But there's no grave to go and see.
Was he killed? Neglected? Was there an accident?

No one mentions it, and all the pictures
have been misplaced, toys given away, papers burned,
and now we're scattered, vengeful, set against
each other, demonstrating in the streets, the past

against the New World. Brother with your blatant blemish,
Sister rejected with your shameful defect—nothing
remains of you but silence, some soot, and emptiness,
a train car of emptiness for every square meter of earth.

49. Euromaidan

To Yuri Andrukhovych

What else is there to tell? That they use fire to defend
themselves against the winter dark. The city burns,
so they take flesh and blood and build a second
city inside, with walls of breath. If winter turns

away, the tsar will wage his war against the protesters
with metal tanks, false words, and heaps of cash.
And there are those who lead a naked man into the snow
and beat him, whistle, put a broom into his hand

and coo: just try to Hetman us, you Cossack. Then they order
him to pose in their selfies with tarry smoke and brown
smudges on snow, staunch proportions in the background.
Then there's that moment in the morgue

when, after several hours, all the cellphones
placed on the blood-stained table in the hall
suddenly began to ring at once, showing the call,
the same word flashing on every screen: Mom.

50. An Act of Speech

By now it's clear what I've inherited—
this great open plain that suddenly gives way
to the steppe without warning, just beyond
the river, traces of campfires, bottles, charred remains,

and many well-worn paths of escape, tank-rutted
tracks where people were chased away and rooms
to live in built exclusively from what
another left, from emptiness. A vacancy, but whose?

With a crowd of new tenants nesting there and living
as nomads camped out at the gates, and a crowd of subjects
claiming their right to this rust, this dug-up pit,
these bulrushes, crevices, thistles tainted

with radium, polonium, cesium. So many subjects
demanding a voice in the sentiments, in this act
of speech made by screaming geese, in the slightest
sigh of wind, moan of tree, ache of the earth.

51. Lacki Brzeg, Ukraine

Today a storm rolls over Lacki Brzeg
and draws the curtain of dust aside: a truck
crawls upward, suddenly a flash of mirror
in motion, then the steppe where those enormous

hot furnaces go on working, continually smelting
time, just like with iron or steel made into fencing
and wire, tracks, posts, a railway bridge, a dog tag
to wear around the neck. When you descend,

you'll see how many of them are rusting there,
along the shore, in hawthorn and night-scented stock.
A few dogs warm themselves on the white cement.
I have high hopes in this inheritance: I will return here

one day in June or May, move in again, become
a part of this landscape, a fragment, hiding amid
the beans on poles, the rows of short sunflowers,
the dog field, the industrial plant, its ruins.

52. In the Cave

We are, after all, never just one nationality,
so let's settle it for once—this choice we have,
our mongrel love, not for a people but a language
of marks, cascade of consonants, signs of incongruity,

a tattoo flush with blood at night if seen
in a certain light: just as with love, the most striking
thing is that which knows how to hide
from the beast of the nation, a one-eyed beast

to whom it answers: nobody, nothing, never,
for no one, from nowhere and nobody's.
And there, where we once brought our love,
an apple tree is blooming. Back then, we could see

love's limp, how it kept falling, then finally soared up
to become a spark in the ether. You said: we can't stay.
Wind ripped my breath, like a damp scarf, from my lungs
and smeared the ripples on the river as it turned away.

53. Revenge Bank

Let's say you've won—some future revolution
and redistribution of goods, with all the oppressed
eagerly writing laws. Representative government.
Justice at last in how to allocate our pain,

the presidential couple promising good fortune.
Lieutenant Anielewicz tracks down all profiteers,
perverts, saboteurs. It takes some years.
Then someone streetside chucks a stone again.

At night again in the market square a crowd,
irate, manipulated, still at evil's beck and call?
Education's useless when enemies crest the hill,
except for engineering, apart from these banal

reports, routine injections, isolation, or the pulse
of an electric collar, a trip somewhere far away,
with a black and white expanse, a flapping sky,
and just beyond the bars, a sea that drinks the voice.

54. SQUIGGLE

For Joseph Brodsky

You write it, *freedom,* and straight from the Polish
alphabet a swarm of parasites begins to surge,
a flock of sooty flecks, clinging to letters,
and they start rustling, buzzing, twisting

the typeface, smacking their lips, making words
grimace, a monkey face: Ą, Ż, Ć. And the sentence
printed from a Roman negative has grown a whole cluster
of tails, turning it from dictum to rant,

a shade, a laugh, an echo. They rattle and dance
at night, and all your monologues become irrelevant,
but this is what letters placed on white attract,
the bristles they grow, how they wake up pregnant,

and suddenly in place of a conclusion
you see some other thing, some shadow traffic
pulsing in hand gestures, hip thrusts, all of existence
in accents, crinkum-crankum, nick-nacks.

55. My Consultants

Due to the dawn and what's going on in this room,
the question of the next election flies under the radar,
and I see, as you well know, how things get dark
whenever we must choose from just a few

of those who want to go and get themselves elected.
I've seen things darkly ever since I started differentiating
between words, taking that shadow color and placing
it on a screen or on a piece of paper like a silhouette

puppet of the hand. The matter of choice
is consequently part of grammar and certain
tastes we need not even try to explain
to ourselves—there's no need. An inner voice

from nowhere. Intersecting coffee rings that circle
words on a page are wiser than any vote cast today.
If I endorse their choice, they'll establish a holiday
for declaiming verses as alcohol is served.

56. Warsaw Was Raw

Just when they thought there would be no repeat
of the nightmare no one wanted to believe—
the past, its bloody pulp, buried right below
the surface, somewhere in the yard, so shallow—

they stopped believing, too, since hell only happens
to those who believe. In place of what took place
they'd take a peaceful life, if only for the sake
of the children, just one quiet, simple old age

in this corner of the world. But who could make
the trade? Was it time, god, satan? Perhaps that brute
who manifests at dawn in the mirror, who uses
familiar words but backward, askew, breaking

them down to letters? However gruesome
the nightmare was, the next will be much worse.
Their calendar said March, their century said twenty-first,
the sky was gray, the sheen and shade of iron.

57. Demolition

So many planks and bricks, tiles and roofing,
the dust gets into everything. A phantom demolition.
This used to be a building, bricks with inscriptions
now unreadable. Black rags and bolts, no proof

that color once existed here. And dust gets in.
The nests of ants and mice now totally exposed.
A moving out, an exodus. This once was home.
Once light and heat and fire. Now so much wind.

And so much soot and dirt. Splinters that pierce the skin.
The tearing down went quickly. Now our children
will roam, nomadic and living on the run.
Refugees blackened with stigma. And dust gets in

to everything. Soot-eaten flesh, air-driven splinters,
dark birth-marked race. So many ghosts in the open.
Meanwhile, the wind peels flesh from white bone,
and the rattling skeleton dances past the horizon.

58. Two Days' Time

Two days, and it will be the sixteenth winter.
I dreamt you walked upstairs yourself and said
that everything was fine now with your leg, you had
a new doctor who was treating you in a modern

high-tech hospital. Your youthful look conveyed
real happiness. And though I knew that it
must be a lie, I laughed, I laughed, and then a bit
like an idiot, I turned my head away

so that you wouldn't see. Of course you'd brought
a present for each of the children—but you stood
by the door, had to get back—and of course I couldn't
touch you at all. I woke as if I'd been caught

and fished out of a stream. The winter sun
pierces right through my eyelid like a needle,
placing there a stud made of ice that will melt
in two days, five, a week from now, a month.

59. The Third Planet

A river's twists, the tarnished crown of luster
above the bank, a meadow burned by winter's breath—
I come here on behalf of this world's nature,
its stunning attribute that it never preserves

today by making tomorrow wear the same dress.
Beyond the shore are chimneys altering the heat,
a sash of smoke above the grass, a spider's web
in which we wade. This evening. Below our feet

are five huge cisterns to amass all the time
evaporating—most acute today. The river turns,
flashes and in one fell swoop steals half the sky,
the color in your eyes. This evening. Only stars:

scales on lash and lid. To get consciousness
plus mortality in a single package, what a joke.
I say this in the dead of winter, on this globe
third from the Sun, spinning within the abyss.

60. Rhythm, Order, and Position

And after a week of ritual dances in the kitchen
and on the stairs, in ballrooms with masked hollow men,
the horror remains that everything's been in vain,
and it only seemed we could break free in the end

from ye olde dualism, only seemed air's memory
did not preserve depressions left by bodies,
no question of half-existence, just an *is* or *is not*,
no shadow mirrored on the photosensitive plate

of summer, just close the drapes to make the positive
appear, developed. Yes, I'm truly dancing,
trying to loosen up these numbed out vacancies
a bit, these murky spheres, these flecks of chaos,

since what matters is the rhythm in which you find
or lose them, the order in which they come into contact
with you, the trace of each position that, in spite of time,
the body stores, heals over, takes care of, looks after.

61. Distillery

The bust went down without a hitch, this means promotion.
They caught him in the act, distilling the molten
molasses of moans, grunts, runny sermons,
warm murmurs and cries into such tiny snippets,

letter by letter in the furnace, his distillery.
They nabbed him drunk. He'd tried the flavor
on his tongue, nonstop strings of dripping letters
all summer, September, almost October...

He also urged the opposite sex to partake,
libation leading to an orgy with the extras,
the house becoming a den. And now forensics
inspects, collects, examines their chemical structures.

Evidence seized: several hundred letters.
But what they're worth, these chains, braids, tangles,
will only be shown in time. For time's the only winner.
Lieutenant Anielewicz has already been promoted to colonel.

62. Even Now

Winter doesn't want to end in some familiar place.
The meadow past the river creaks, in the tunnel there's ice,
even beyond the warehouse where time collects dust
winter is still holding out, most fiercely inside of us.

It's so insatiable, it strips the city bare of excess
and color, of grass, cafés, the scent of women, dresses,
disrobes the wall and in it makes a gash,
a few months pass, above the chimney, smoke and ash.

All through the night they feed it with salt trucks,
things taste so bland we have to scatter in some ache,
may it remain, otherwise we'll simply fall asleep,
no one will keep watch, no one will blaspheme.

And no one will be sitting here under a blown
bulb, nervously arranging words against this season,
like sharpening a knife on endings and rhymes till they bleed,
though winter has no heart—you have to stab your own.

63. The Crisis of the Polish State

Pologne c'est un pays marecageux ou habitent les Juifs

This thrush that sings at two a.m. outside
our window in the parking lot has saved
the day, the month. But think what kind of route
it's flown to end up here—past those depraved

hunters of birds in the groves of Cyprus, past Russian
fighter jets in Syria, dioxin clouds above Ploesti,
the pesticide-polluted Danube, tainted waste by the tons
in forests lining the Oder—through all this debris

just to soar over to Poland, where a rubbish faction
has just sprung up in Warsaw. Here it's bitter
cold and the clouds hang low, and all this rain
for a week has turned the patchy, trash-littered lawn

into a paddy fit for rice. So, thanks for coming and
proclaiming your dominion with such amorous
song in the night above this boggy land
where Jews have vanished. Count me among your serfs.

64. Wind

Thanks for the years, the ten most beautiful
that possibly could happen here, if viewed
from somewhere up above, an airborne satellite's
perspective—still the same old Eastern Europe,

best place to disappear, one generation
after the next, leaving behind what's mostly gone,
town squares in ruins, archives only partly there,
boots strewn about, stray combs and hair, hair

everywhere, and all the broken reading glasses,
prosthetic limbs now useless, cartons, crates, suitcases,
handbags, attachés, empty cans and vials,
boxes with nothing left to put inside,

that carry nothing but air, an ocean
of air that, if released in a single motion,
would form a wind so great, it would carry us off
above the trees and out above the rooftops.

65. STONE

A flooded meadow across the river,
gardens no one has entered for years.
The stroke was grim, left one entire
side of the body dead, closed off an eye

to the light. And words are so unclear
when they're pronounced, we even have to guess
which language. Lack of feeling in the fingers.
Is that smiling or pulling a face?

The ashen, burnt-out grass and rags deposited
by current, papers wind-blown this way—
I thought the body dead, a thing to one day
fall off, perhaps today. But not quite yet,

since someone slept there yesterday, left garbage.
Slight tremor of a finger, micro-twitch of eye.
To live with a stone, a heavy stricken part
into which immortality slips so easily.

66. What About Him?

I wish you were here—I've set up my life
in this void filled to the brim with your absence.
And maybe the mystery lies in precisely
this fact—the world sprung into existence

the moment you withdrew, leaving only the echo
of a shriek, abandoned clothes, abandoned space,
and a dog who all year runs into the road
to the spot where he saw you last—inside the gate

where trash collects, with its crumpled ball
of a partial list of what to buy, what to fix,
what to give away, what number to call. Fantastic
vacation plans. I'll charge you double for the ticket

to cover the return. Meanwhile the pooch,
what does he do, what's his status between
A and B, will he be enticed by a whiff, a clue
from the forest, the snow, the world beyond this street?

III. Summer of Music

67. Summer of Music

And what am I to do with such a message?
I use binoculars to survey what's been lost.
No one to prop up the house and garden rotting,
one wing gone numb, moss spreading along the edges

and up the stairs, blurring inscriptions. As if written
in a foreign language, words are missing letters
stolen by locals. Behind the linden, graffiti
and broken bottles—our boys were here,

searching for gold, rooting through springtime,
prying apart the walls and floors. I would move in,
but a certain credit card keeps getting refused—
perhaps our benevolent sponsor changed their mind.

What if, instead, we bring power out to the garden,
hang lanterns in the orchard, put up tables,
spend the summer on music, sex, libation?
No need to reply—all you have to do is shine.

68. Sorting

We started with the mending of the world
at night, under the stairwell, sorting the interspersed
rubbish into bins, the junk we hoarded
from distant times, trash from the best and worst

of years, split up in piles: first, empty bottles,
as those who drank with us have long since turned
to gas glowing for a moment above a shot glass—
happiness lasts a second before it burns.

Second, paper, all the trees fallen to do this
scribbling: so many words and strokes
to write it down and blur the abyss
from far away, in the hotel, before the light goes out.

And third, what once was alive but now has perished,
the waste produced between us when my body
tries stubbornly to reach your body there
at a distance greater than two galaxies.

69. WHY

Did time begin? And when exactly was
our separation? Where did this edict
come from, that life arises by subtracting
things from a starting number (one of which is love)?

And why is time a number that knows only
negative equations? Why does a cloud vanish
behind the forest, beyond the window, why but a flash
of deer going past the train, why finally

does everything you want to keep go missing.
What point is there to fire, illumined faces
circled round, if darkness soon replaces
them, dismissed, doused? I'd like to donate all this

memory to someone, give away this enormous
chaotic force that comes on suddenly like a flood
or stroke, marking the body with signs of oblivion,
part statement, part fear, total paralysis.

70. SCENT

The all-night shops. And all my life suspended
at the threshold, part in the dark, among the broken
dishes and hardened traces of blood—night a relay station
transmitting cries and grunts—and there at the entrance

faces with squinting eyes, trying to read
the names on bottles, narcotics, cigarettes,
looking for dried herbs they will need
for transmutation in the attic, to pupate on the quiet

before the auroras come up. Life at the threshold.
Trying to pronounce words, their jumble of letters,
something like a kind of wail escapes the throat,
a howl each night from over the ridge. A hunger

seethes in dark regions, but there's nothing
to buy to satiate it. Inexplicable scent,
unfamiliar labels. Over the shoulder, dim city,
then river, calamus, thickets where animals shift.

71. FORMULA

And even the Great Collider's just one enormous
camera, thousands of metric tons, with shutter
set and ready to catch the gremlin of this world
in the act, red-handed, the moment when someone

let's slip a piece of detail, and there's no
turning back, everything continuing on its own
according to a string of formulas recorded
in squeaky chalk on the blackboard.

In front of you, four seats ahead, a girl,
her back focused on being the only one
in the whole universe, the shape of such
a left ear, nape of neck, hair, shoulders, gesture

of half-listening to the squeak on the black expanse
as a hand writes out the signs that herald her
future life: line of rival numbers, rush of letters,
and the moment hovering, right before the answer.

72. Summertime

Do you recall those feral days in the dorm
when time disappeared? And we were driven out
of bed only by our great hunger, after a marathon
of a hundred amorous acts till we lost count

of hours, days, nights. And in the shared kitchen,
we warmed up pasta on the only burner
that worked, trying to divine from the darkened
window if it was Wednesday still or another

Thursday. Somewhere along the way, time changed
to daylight savings, and our small eternity got lost
at the last screening. Boulevards of car exhaust,
then suddenly the scent of spring: forsythia, dogwood—

and more, a toss of your hair? I have no clue
if all this is due to using love or wearing through
the body, or just a trick of one small death
when time, the operator, turns into the parameter.

73. Porta Susa

Why are you suddenly breathing so well?
Just step outside the station with the white Alps
standing there over your shoulder like angels
on guard at the entrance to the garden, or perhaps

like a squad of skiers in camouflage underwear
training their scopes on you, even as you sip espresso.
The breath is deeper here. They say it's a matter
of increased pressure, the sky-high stratified shadows

in layers, the rustle of tunics removed and whispers
still escaping from the stones at night,
air that forms our breath of shredded paper,
a great library that rests on pillars of sky.

The more crowded outside, the more vacant inside seems.
The pressure's low in your flat empty country,
but the body's cramped, layered with scars and dreams,
keepsakes of each age, a paradise of archaeology.

74. The Law of Conservation of Energy

If we're talking opposites, our suffering
must be an act of pleasure for you there,
where you survive by raising a church
of vitality generators, a swarm of chickens, broilers.

A farm on a blue planet? And there's a law
of conservation of energy—after you suck out our life,
the shell remains, and then you squirt some type
of amplifier into a random part of the body.

But I prefer the version where there's nectar
in a cup or a skull. In any case, a scandal—you feed
like some lower being, bug, louse, tapeworm, beetle,
don't you? From my perspective, you're similar

to a parasite. That is, from the perspective of
a hog. There's rain today, from dawn till dusk,
and maybe out of spite we're still under the covers.
And how are you?—here, again, there's love.

75. THE WARMEST PLACE

If spring falls short, then be the spring yourself—
you hold abundant light inside, enough to give warmth
to whatever's within reach and even what's in view:
chair midriff, door slab, icicle knob, room.

Who cares if the Baltic is frozen—a Swedish arctic fox
has found a way across the page of ice to write
a runic greeting on the snow in yellow ink
below the lamppost. The coldest place at home

is the radiator's hip, the thermal plant having closed
long ago, and it's pointless to pin your hopes
on spring. Besides you hold within yourself,
enough fire to make the covers melt right off

and thaw the district to a mile radius,
plus a fair depth, add four more dimension besides.
Just for good measure. For starters. Be springtime,
the grass' green flame, its blood, be April, be sun.

76. ALL-NIGHT SHOPS

Not good with money. Too many coins in the pocket
or maybe it's too few, but that's not vital.
What counts is how the journey goes: four tottering steps
along the garden beds to the gate, avoid the puddle,

the acacia trees, garages, go past the garbage can
into the tunnel, more or less fifty meters in total.
The tail of a rat or a new poster in the dark passage
or springtime: beyond the fence the sudden jazz of
    nightingales,

the panicked flight of sparrows. Ready on the racks:
a quarter loaf, a cube of butter, parsley,
some newspaper headlines, the free weekly,
colorful handbags. And then there's going back:

the same, carefully. Time, as always, is a few steps
behind, too much distracts it: squirming ants, a shred
of gold from a wrapper, the poster's letters read
from this direction, which has the opposite effect.

77. Any number

The banknote where I jotted down your number,
I somehow lost it, must have paid cash for something,
though what would I buy that cost that much?
And now for all eternity I'll be waiting

for it to find its way back to me, either that or counting
on us meeting a second time. Or I could select
digits in random order—leave it to happy accident,
or go out shopping, get cash in different amounts,

or sit in the same spot in the coffee shop
at the airport or the train station and stubbornly watch
the door—and maybe you'll come. It's as much of a shot
as that bill falling out of someone's pocket.

You know how it is with numbers: they never end,
and if they take us away, they'll be no poorer.
At most, they'll grow by the stubbornly absent
negative value at the table in the corner.

78. Second Crisis of the Reader

Today let's get to know the reader.
The worm who lives among these letters.

Once he was a nobody, now he's a king.
He takes a swig and rules over everything.

He has a mission, position, power and clout.
He should have died but didn't know how.

And now, just dream of him, that's enough.
If one person thinks of him, he triumphs.

79. Spring Awakening

What's missing there for you? The spring? The springing
grass from the mud after only one warm evening?
Nightingale, Grackle? All those birds returned from hell?
The finely blooming branches of the Mirabelle?

The sword of sun on concrete wall? Dripping hair
and drenched shoes, a huge downpour
from which to run into the arms of someone else?
That someone else? Just say it: love?

Night, a hundred times I write on the back
of a certain girl the words thank you. In the dark,
the line of her hip shines brighter than Orion's star
there, in the blackest well. Is this what you are

lacking? We lie together in abundant light.
Whoever wanders in this darkness, this cold night,
across deserted space and wastelands, the brightest
star will lead them here: there is life on planet earth.

80. VIRUS

Here on the sand just for you I've written
some words that, by some miracle, survived
this plague, gone rampant in the capital again
amid the multiplying sums, a novel virus

bred from senselessness that spreads to terms, syntax.
How dark the winter! How many working smokestacks
our era has! What smoke they make, released
into the atmosphere with complete impunity

come four o'clock. The greatest threat to the state
of your face is not ash but distraction. You must focus,
remember details: a view of mountain peaks
mirrored on the eyelid, a bay that cradles

your body like a warm embrace. If you can see me,
it means the stove's still lit. I'm feeding it
these moments, one by one. The flame agrees:
I am (life, the hiss of chemistry, the whine of applied physics).

81. Puzzle

Letters. These cutouts of darkness, puzzle of smudges—
at some point I'll run out of them, compose
a conclusive picture at last: abyss, black hole,
the vastness of the cosmos woven out of nothing

but meanings. I'll move there, into the wilds,
right to the very center of the dark, headquarters of loss,
the very place where you are now, or actually are not,
there's no one, nothing. Only words, a hell

of words, a hell of marks. Remember when
we went to see the ocean from the cliff at dusk?
It made a lot of noise and danced, did not succumb
to sleep. A single light in darkness slowly wending

its way, warm skin, a touch, now nothing, happiness
turned ash. What's left is slight, so slight I must arrange
the pieces carefully to make this negation,
this mournful shroud, scrap by scrap by scrap.

82. Features

And if you do exist—say it—are you not living
somewhere inside of me at times? Unfurling like fungus,
a lump, a foreign body, cosmic cancer, stardust,
from day to day, from year to year, invading

my territory, seizing land, inciting a coup
one day at dawn in winter. Then you'll rule
with absolute power inside my body thanks to
advancements in conversion surgery to morph into

your likeness, which means nothing, right? If you exist
you are an enemy within, my own antithesis,
an agent, saboteur, and every night you ingest
another bite of me, am I right? It's no coincidence

that every morning in the glass I see more traces
of pretense creeping in and diagnose my face
as having someone else's features, wrinkles, grit,
a foreign sentence added, but not in my own script.

83. Piazza del Nettuno

Here there is so much light that people flee
from it into porticoes, dungeons, shutters, the shade
of cypress and stone ravines that lead through the streets.
It's called putting off what cannot be escaped:

standing naked in the light. The squinting eye
only opens in the dark and straight away begins
drawing on the walls, on surfaces and sides
and curves, on the planes of the face, hip, abdomen

a view from memory, projecting a picture
of its own solitude, but also what kind of parts
make up this world, what kind of objects are fixtures.
It's easier to see what's missing in the dark.

That's why espresso is black and paper is white,
so white it glares, and if the vision of humans
is to withstand it, these letters are vital,
a splash of the devil's juice on the angel's dress.

84. An Unexpected Turn of Events

A sudden shock of rain in Bologna that pours
quite literally just like a storm on the frigid sea
way up North. Scarcely a drop and it instantly
devastates the plan on the face of a tourist,

furrows with skill the up-to-now concealed
map of the homeland: clear cuts, pastures, barren tracts,
a swollen storm front looming above the atlas,
a tractor meant for rescue stuck up to its axle.

The legs of a girl who happens to be sheltering
by chance under this same colonnade—
from atop her knee a drop admires the leg's cascade,
a spyglass sent from heaven by our great voyeur.

The drop reflects what he demands of the world,
everything set in a dance under the stars,
but only briefly—according to the laws of gravity,
the daisies await the drop impatiently.

85. ROUTE

So as not to call out to you, not to address you
by any name, instead we summon death.
The two of you are one. That missing screw
of the machine, rusting in a field of flower beds

with poppies and chamomile; that vast expanse left
after extraction of atoms, hadrons, bosons;
that number yielded from the aggregate
of phone numbers; those four forgotten

lines from a poem that came back in a dream tonight.
How quickly the space left by a body gives up its heat
to hands, face, clothing, and finally the air,
and straight away the place grows cold as objects

lying about: that half-drunk cup of tea, the mirror
filled up with want, the strand of hair curling toward
the drain like the Silk Road through the Karakum
known as Tartary, the wall that defends the void.

86. Reverse

If you are the reverse, why so many urgent
conflicts inside of me, these empty spaces,
this meat, this other me, a double agent
who's running down the clock and wasting

seconds by the day, working through the night,
reliving double, triple lives, and yet another
while I'm dead to the world, before I rise
adding them quickly to the total number

of years, turning the meter, depositing lime
in veins and stones in kidneys, laying down
materials for building a monument lined
in bricks from within. That's why at dawn

the texture of skin in the mirror is like cement,
even marble in spots, and there's a strange dryness
to the tongue, resistance in the voice before it hardens
the whirling, rolling, crushing, grinding inside.

87. In the Bushes

An insect swarm in tamarisk,
a sign we're close to summer's bliss.

Let's take a trip into the thicket.
Life, if you want, can be this basic.

Slim chance we'll get another one.
I've popped the cork, the bottle's open.

May I remember you like this.
Deep in the grass, with a sprig of mint.

88. A Glass

Five days I polish the stones of the city with the soles
of my shoes, where time likewise has honed trajectory
and carved its name in footfall zigzags of an era,
features of presence, body shape, a face in profile.

Now seen from up above the city's just a coin
with which to buy a ticket from the conductor
or one shot of espresso. I close the lids of my eyes,
and the world still exists: below the table sparrows

fight for a crust of bread and kids on bikes
race around the square and from the open cathedral
silence emerges, stretches, stretches its spine in the sunlight.
Even the colors are probably still bright

there, where they were. Everything composed
in signs of absence. Here, on the table, I'll set
this poem for you like an empty glass so all
you have to do is bring some wine to fill it.

89. This Dog's Life

On four Greek islands and along the twists
of the three great rivers of the North, I've written
a name. To read it, you must hover a bit,
but don't you know how to fly? A winged spirit,

a seraph, a seagull, a crane, or Daedalus,
British Air, or some more complicated mode
of levitation, completely foreign to me. The first
mutt you'll see on the street will be me, as I wrote

once before. I'll follow everywhere you go,
even if you wend your way into the maze
of alleys, I'll be on your scent as it grows
stronger, more you. For now, I'm still here, lazing

in the square below the arches, and this summer
is so enormous that I live but in its margins:
by day, dozing in the shade of students' skirts,
by night, howling at the stars to let me in.

90. Outside Prudnik

Well, you're not here. You're far away, remote,
somewhere that's nowhere, perhaps outside Prudnik
or in some kind of fourth field, parking lots
and mall still visible. And in this nowhere universe

there are no hours or minutes, just the now
in which you live, if you, indeed, have what I'm missing.
And that's exactly what I'm missing. Now
means never, right? You're never nowhere—that is

how it goes, forgive the rebus. You being out
of time only serves me well for the time being.
I bought tobacco. Here, light up and fill with smoke
so I can see your outline, tender boundary

where you begin. Do you believe it's possible
to die for love? To go beyond, outside Prudnik
by motorcycle, curve upon curve downhill.
If you believe, then take this death as keepsake.

91. Backpack

This world, along with several other worlds,
can fit into the outside pocket of my backpack
or in a shopping bag from a little boutique
in Switzerland with a view over the roof, the lake,

the Alps, eternity, the teeth of the hungry maw
still open. Watch me now, how I'm dancing around
with a bottle on my head and glasses in my paws.
No matter the size of my steps, I'll arrive too soon.

With time, I'll lose as much as the distance I cover,
to die in combat, what an honor. Sorry for the casualties.
I tried to carry it with care, to see what I could save,
got drunk so as not to spill a drop. My right leg's tricky.

This world, along with other worlds in the set,
this worm food falling from my outside pocket,
crow food, mold food, spilling out with coins
for buying wine and seashells found in Spain.

92. NEVER

Never have I found you more beautiful than now.
Look—we're being hunted, yet still we walk around.
In front of us a road in the dust, a lively sea.
A life that turned out as I dreamed it would be.

93. Shadow

To you, I leave the places where I'm absent.
That one along the Oder, another at the Reservoir,
apart from those some beds and attics, a mattress.
Especially the mattress. It'll be so much easier

to think of you as filling them, growing and going
rampant in places vacated and those that still remain,
to say it plain—everywhere else. From the shadows
perhaps you're watching me pass through the gate

and snap, I'm gone, no longer. I bequeath to you
what falls apart, burns down, what shifts in shape,
what changes its own state, what's been consumed
in the grave by a fat worm and is already clay

and grass and wood and chamomile. Please live there
and use it how you want, climb into my clothes and put
yourself in my shoes, set up a table, drink with the neighbors.
It's my word, my letters against your minutes.

94. What Makes No Motion?

So, what remains? Coffee in a cup, breadcrumbs
on the table, garlic clove and lemon wedge, the hum
of a road, the bed in which a body breaks down
to pulp, phosphates, sulfur and carbon compounds,

the soul escaping through holes, that is, there's gas
of an unpleasant odor soaking into curtain fabric,
rugs, upholstery. How difficult to clear
the air in a home! Only unfinished rows of letters

are dead, but luckily the page holds blanks,
some bits of space not yet filled up with marks.
So much goes on in them! If there's no motion,
it must be the letters. Stumbling up their rungs,

the drunken moonlight tries to climb inside.
It's very, very beautiful—Lieutenant Anielewicz
sets down his autopsy tools: the saw, the forceps,
the scissors, and sings an old, old tune, touched deeply.

95. The Cave of the Nymphs

And then the body carried aloft on the high seas
is covered by the morphology of its journey,
soon it will be hard to distinguish sense from sign,
food from consumer, breathing out from breathing in.

Travelling companions and parasitic lichen,
white-breasted Nereids, squadrons of Sirens,
songs of the Tritons. There go the atolls, the flicker
of Fortunate Isles in froth on the buffering shore.

Cape Fear and Cape of Good Illusion,
Dantean Island. A returning surge, Neptune
is pulling up the nets of tangled currents,
and in the flooded caves a dowry is left.

As for form, it's also along for the ride
and always bears a resemblance to something else,
in length, depth, and the last two measurements
fulfilling the template of a body divine.

96. The Divine Comedy

The melody from a theremin, heard at night
that one and only time, instantly forgotten
on the plane as soon as the ugly stewardess
standing in the aisle began her pantomime,

that dance of gestures, hand signs, throwing over you
like a sorceress a heavy curtain of weariness,
a miracle of amnesia to carry you to the end
of the world cleansed, faint, in a stupor,

awakened from hypnosis. You can see the scene
but cannot hear the sound: an air harp played
by a musician without a voice on the rays
of the sun, and pigeons whirling in a nervous sheen,

and sunlight flooding the square, casting its gold
on all the windows of the city, indeed how royal,
so every passer-by remembers the comedy,
as if farewell is meant for all eternity.

97. Second Poem for Menelik

I won't be coming after all, letters are swarming
my body, crawling like earwigs, leeches.
An itchy rash, forgive my useless scratching.
And training doesn't help, standing in formation,

infantry songs—I sort them into ranks
of foreign-sounding quotes and watch them go to war—
they bite each other some but bite me more.
They die faster than sunlight, but the strength

of my allergy intensifies when they return at night,
so I collect them one by one and chain them up
like galley slaves, stanza by stanza, hundred
by hundred on a paper ship. They'll be quite

handy for you, I've heard, in your master plan, useful
for digging your black hole. Inside this envelope
I send no punctuation, just a sprig of mint that I broke
off yesterday, a sign the world remains shockingly beautiful.

98. THE TRAIL GOES COLD

Lieutenant, I regret to report the trail's gone cold
in the clover by the river, a quarter orange,
the shape of es and zee in trampled grass, silhouettes
of letters facing each other. Accent marks adorn

their tops, a trace of skulls? The water's black
and deep and murky from a factory still churning
on the other side, letting off prions. I've ransacked
everything, but there's nothing, no messages or words.

Perhaps they'll surface lower down the weir
or get caught in a turbine. Or when spring comes,
releasing ice, they'll be carried out to sea.
Or maybe, just maybe, it's all a delusion

since nothing round here seems suspicious,
not even one small fox or den of mice,
only the acacia's crazy fragrance,
and it's not yet in bloom on either side.

99. Open

Judging by the signs of struggle, busted
furniture, traces of blood, these small bite marks,
it must have been love, Lieutenant. The trail
leads past the gas station to the empty tract

behind the factory. I'd recognize love anywhere,
if only by its scent. Last summer I drove it
out to the ocean, and the whole car reeked.
And even now I sense it. All the way home

it kept on moaning and whining there in the back,
until I let it out at night. Forty-five stitches
and a scar, but still standing. And I won't make
the same mistake twice. I've got a semi-automatic

shotgun and some extra ammunition.
It can survive on dust but won't get far
alone and in the end must come to someone.
I'll leave the kitchen light on and the door partly—

Afterword

"The lyric is a voice uttered by someone in the moment
when they realize they are not immortal."
—Tomasz Różycki

I.

Growing up, Tomasz Różycki believed that he was only
temporarily living in Silesia and would soon return to
heaven. In this case, heaven was the city of Lwów, which
his family mentioned daily. When the borders of Poland
shifted west after World War II, they were forcibly reset-
tled to the Silesian region of Poland, to the town of Opole,
where Różycki was born. But they kept pre-war Lwów alive
in idealized memories, a kind of mirror world to daily life in
their new home.[1]

In memory, at least, life went on in that other city un-
changed by the war and communist times. Stepping
through the looking glass, those displaced could be re-
united with a second self left behind, if only in the intangible
realm of recollection. The work of other twentieth-century

Polish poets from the periphery, such as Czesław Miłosz, Adam Zagajewski, and Zbigniew Herbert, speaks to this kind of exile's longing, constructed from the tension between presence and absence.

Tangible, physical reminders of absence were everywhere. Empty factories and machines turning to rust in a field. Contaminated waste dumped by the Soviet army along the Oder River. Chimney stacks belching smoke above vacant ruins—material reminder of the war and the Jewish population no longer there, never to be named. Różycki's childhood made him a poet of this layered communal history, with an awareness of successive catastrophes across Eastern Europe and an acute sense that something was missing.[2]

2.

These "Settings"—to use the title of one of his poems—inform the contemporary world of *To the Letter*, published in 2016 against the backdrop of rising authoritarianism across eastern Europe and a struggle between liberal and conservative paradigms in Poland. "Now we're scattered, vengeful, set against each other," Różycki writes, "demonstrating in the streets, the past against the New World." It's the same old curse, the same old dynamic that keeps repeating across generations, something absent that no one mentions, traces left behind that fuel society's feuds.

In this poem, Różycki has in mind Hellinger's idea of "family constellations" and "systemic entanglements" caused by unresolved trauma. The poem performs a kind of psychotherapeutic naming of the dynamic: Mother, Father, Neighbor who denounced the children (now gone) as Jewish. A constellation with emptiness at its center. The collection as a whole draws heavily on the lexicon of astronomy as a way to name this dynamic of the family constellation, with a black hole at its center, the "headquarters of loss," as he says in another poem.

Trauma is a vacuum, and this book is Różycki's theory of what it means to inherit the void.

3.

Of course, the void is also where we will all return one day. The author, forty-six at the time of the book's publication, writes from an amplified awareness of his own mortality and the passing away of previous generations. We glimpse the moment of his father's passing in "To Give Water to the Thirsty" and hear about a dream in which his mother returns on the sixteenth anniversary of her death in "Two Days' Time." With them go firsthand memories of heavenly

Lwów, though the speaker still has high hopes in this inheritance and plans, however futilely, to return, as we learn in "Lacki Brzeg, Ukraine."

There's also a sense of mourning past versions of a younger, more virile self. Whether it be accepting the hardened texture of skin that's now like cement in "Reverse" or recalling "those feral days in the dorm / when time disappeared" in "Summertime," these poems relate traces of private memory from the perspective of someone acutely aware of his age.

But we don't get a lot of specific detail in these personal memories, presented as a kind of cipher impossible to decode without the help of the poet himself (given to me often, thankfully, during the translation process). This is what makes Różycki's poetry so different from the American post-confessional lyric. There's no desire for intimate revelation or delving into internal complications that come from private psychological experience. Instead, these poems are interested in observing the economy of loss in which we're all engaged as a kind of operational mode— loss both in term of collective memory and in terms of the material realm.[3] In this way, tension comes not from the personal but from the philosophical investigation of the dialectic of presence and absence in which we're all inscribed.

4.

Quoting other poets becomes an important strategy for Różycki in building a sense of what's absent, much like building up the border of a dark hole makes it visible. He joins other writers, entangles his lines with theirs.

From the very first poem, Różycki writes alongside Debora Vogel's *Acacias Blooming*, a montage novel about Lwów that in large part reads like prose poetry. Known as "the wandering star" of Polish and Yiddish modernist literature, Vogel serves as a kind of guide for a wandering speaker in *To the Letter* who is trying to give shape to "ungainly space." Similarly, Vogel writes:

> There's an enormous amount of space in this world.
>   Unnecessary, ungainly space…
> Space as boring as people with lives lost. Weighty
>   space, like a fateless life. Spaces
> that squeeze out big empty tears. For no one.
>   There's too much space in this world.
> We have to do something with the artless space of
>   the world.[4]

In Różycki's poems, we encounter just such an excess of empty, endless, abandoned, deserted space left behind after the warmth of a body has ceased to exist. What should we do with it? Perhaps, as in the poem "When Do Acacias Bloom?" we can be like a seed and soar up across this emptiness, to replant somewhere, begin the process of growth that fills the void. Of course, with such textual echoes, we're reminded also of the absence of Vogel herself, shot in the Lwów ghetto in 1942.

5.

"How I wish you were here"—a longing that gains momentum each time the refrain repeats throughout this collection. We're meant to hear multiple voices. There's Roger Waters singing about his friend Syd Barrett's mental breakdown in Pink Floyd's "Wish You Were Here." There's also Joseph Brodsky writing in English in his poem "A Song," "I wish you were here, dear. / I wish you were here," ending with the pertinent lines: "What's the point of forgetting / if it's followed by dying?"[5] And there's Stanisław Barańczak translating "A Song" into Polish and then writing his own poem called "I Wish You Were Here." This intimate phrase, through layers of quotation, becomes a universal expression of loneliness and loss.

Barańczak's entire collection *A Postcard from This World* in which his poem appears serves as another guide for *To the Letter.* [6] Różycki starts "the mending of the world / at night, under the stairwell, sorting the interspersed / rubbish into bins," much like Barańczak writes of "throwing trash into the abyss" in his poem "Taking the Garbage Cans to the Curb." Or, look up Barańczak's poem "Some Kind of You" and the way that it calls out to "my interlocutor, Professional Psychotherapist, Gracious Reader, Doppelganger Straining in Vain for the Last Forty Two Years to Hear."[7] Both poets, in middle age, acutely aware of an "I" and an "anti-I" that long for each other across the abyss.

6.

"How I wish you were here"—a calling out for an absent hero, someone, anyone who might be able to rescue twenty-first-century human beings from the history that informs our present and already has designs on our future. In this way, we're also meant to hear multiple addressees. Certainly, in *To the Letter* there's a sense of calling out to an angelic messenger, though it's important to note that god for Różycki, unlike for Barańczak, is always lower case. If these poems are prayer or apostrophe to god, they are couched as intimate conversation meant not to ridicule the sacred but to thwart pathos.[8] Rather than blasphemy, the familiar tone brings out irony as a form of emotional defense.

These poems also call out to an absent beloved, and eroticism charges the longing for presence. If only you were here, we'd "strip down a bit more, lie naked / at the brink of an era, shocked by love." But the lover remains at a remove, while the poetic "I" (assigned a masculine gender) writes to her in the middle of the night, aroused but perpetually alone. Love—a feminine noun in Polish—takes on the form of a fantastical creature, half immortal and capable of metamorphosis, half animal—like a dog or some more feral beast—elusive and dangerous.[9] It represents a wholeness that can never be maintained in our mortal incarnation. And time keeps track of the separation between the mortal and immortal, since "life arises by subtracting / things from a starting number (one of which is love)."

Yet a third possibility for the "you" is poetic self-address, a speaking back to the "anti-I" or doppelganger or second self, located somewhere else. If these poems long for an absent hero, they both raise and cast doubt on the idea that the poet could be such a hero. They dismantle the myth of the poet as priest and poetry as a gateway to the sacred.[10] In this way, *To the Letter* explores the crisis of poetic articulation and picks apart language, down to its most basic element of letters. The poet appears rather helpless against words, which insist on "running toward the paper's edge, holding / each other's endings right before they jump" into the void.

Różycki cannot build a coherent narrative from his inheritance of elusive memories and abandoned objects. At most, he participates through allusion and quotation in the weaving of a layered poetic fabric, impossible to disentangle or use to establish a reliable understanding. Instead, he recognizes the abilities and limitations of language, given its multiplicity and plurality of signification.

7.

Which is where rhyme comes in. Rhyme requires a writer (and a translator, for that matter) to privilege sound over sense. The way Różycki uses it, often slantly and in variable order, rhyme works to further destabilize the text as a definitive articulation and functions as both incantation and play. Chimes and repetitions and puns add to affect, which is important for Różycki. They work against the intensity of his erudite persona, chipping away at the sophistication of his intertextual web and adding to the emotional defense of his carefree, familiar, ironic tone. We're only playing here, "trying to loosen up these numbed out vacancies / a bit, these murky spheres, these flecks of chaos" through "Rhythm, Order, and Position"—a title that echoes Democritus' atomistic void hypothesis of the universe and adds to the ongoing humor of a deliberately naïve dialogue with presocratic philosophy.

8.

Translating a book of poetry interested in stripping language down to its very building blocks of letters poses certain unique challenges. Polish uses the Roman alphabet, but with nine special characters: ą – ć – ę – ł – ń – ó – ś – ź – ż. Those tails and accents and strokes represent the instability of language for Różycki. He interrogates this instability in the poem "Squiggle," which also parallels a section of Joseph Brodsky's poem "A Part of Speech": "and when 'the future' is uttered, swarms of mice /rush out of the Russian language and gnaw a piece / of ripened memory which is twice / as hole-ridden as real cheese."[11] In Różycki's poem, this swarm of mice becomes a swarm of diacritics: "You write it, *freedom,* and straight from the Polish / alphabet a swarm of parasites begins to surge, / a flock of sooty flecks, clinging to letters."

Despite these orthographic differences, a reader easily enough can pick up on Różycki's allusion to Roland Barthes' well-known book *S/Z* when they come across a poem titled "Ż/Ś" or encounter these two letters in the collection's imagery, such as "the shape of es and zee in trampled grass, silhouettes / of letters facing each other" in "The Trail Goes Cold." Barthes' ideas, both in *S/Z* and his famous essay "The Death of the Author," resonate broadly with Różycki's themes. Barthes' emphasis on the multiple layers and meanings that an individual reader brings to interpreting a text informs the textual fabric Różycki, in the role of reader himself, weaves from scraps of other texts, a style that many Polish critics describe as a multilayered palimpsest.

But what about the diacritics that adorn the Ż/Ś, those accents and tails that "twist [the Polish] script to a devilish / grimace, a caricature"? They have a special importance here. If you add the diacritics in Polish, then they align neatly with the words for life (Ż for życie) and death (Ś for śmierć)—an alchemy sadly lost in English. This is probably why Różycki switches the letters around, so that life comes before death. And, like in Barthes equation of two opposing protagonists, the slash represents opposition, the contrast between two constants. A mirror.

It might be helpful to add here that the inverse of the death of the author is the life of the text. Różycki plays with this mirror effect, turning the relationship between writer and reader on its head. In "First Crisis of the Reader," for example, instead of Czesław Miłosz's famous pronouncement that "poems should be written rarely and reluctantly," reading becomes the sacred activity that should be done "rarely and reluctantly." Moreover, to decipher the mystery of the author's death, *To the Letter* follows Lieutenant Anielewicz—a name that relates etymologically to the word for angel—in a quasi plot thread that unfolds like a murder investigation. Who killed the author? Just as Anielewicz follows the clues left on a dead body, we follow the text to discover its code left by someone who was trying to escape the normal course of human life and "outwit necessity" by writing it all down.

9.

Mirrors and the balancing of equations, repetitions and the circulation of meanings. These are the patterns Różycki is interested in uncovering in his poetic bookkeeping, working against a divine force that is trying to "Zero out / our balance sheet, this tango with duality." He owes a debt to many authors, whose words circulate in his poetry just as money circulates in the economy. It's an important principle of collective life, the flow in which words—and the letters that create them like coins make up a dollar—participate.

In this way, he posits for poetry an alternate economy to that of big business, which spreads like a metaphorical plague of nonsense and banality, and which ultimately adds up to nothing. The poem "Virus" (written before Covid) presents the tension between these two economic formulations, with the world of business and media belching words like smoke that kills off any meaning. The irony is that to live also necessitates burning energy, which adds to the smoke. It necessitates spending and losing, the "loss economy" in which we're all engaged. Business, along with god and our own bodies, trying to zero us out. "It's like pollution in the air," he explained to me:

> We have to try not to be dissolved by the smoke. We have to recollect certain brilliant moments of illumination, epiphany, happiness—remember that the world is wonderful. And we have to carry those details. Sometimes, that's how we survive.

Mira Rosenthal
Kraków, 2022

Notes

1. Mira Rosenthal, "A Conversation with Tomasz Różycki," *Music & Literature* (June, 2019), https://www.musicandliterature.org/features/2019/5/27/a-conversation-with-tomasz-rycki.
2. Paulina Żarnecka, "Pamięć ukryta pod ziemią. Porzucone ślady przeszłości w wierszach z tomu Litery Tomasza Różyckiego" in *Obroty liter: Szkice o twórczości Tomasza Różyckiego*, ed. Anna Czabanowska-Wróbel and Magdalena Rabizo-Birek (Kraków: Universitas, 2019), 357.
3. Żarnecka, 348.
4. "Jest ogromnie dużo przestrzeni w świecie. Przestrzeni niepotrzebnej, nieporadnej... Przestrzenie nudne jak ludzie ze straconym życiem. Przestrzenie ciężkie: jak życie bez losu. Przestrzenie, które wyciskają wielkie, puste łzy. I są dla nikogo. Za dużo przestrzeni jest na świecie. Trzeba coś począć z pałubiastą przestrzenią świata." Debora Vogel, *Akacje kwitną* (Kraków: Austeria, 2006), 105.
5. Joseph Brodsky, "A Song," *The New Yorker* (March 27, 1989), 40.
6. Małgorzata Gorczyńska, "Palimpsest, maska, twarz. O Literach Tomasza Różyckiego," in *Obroty liter*, 436.
7. "Mój rozmówco, Fachowy Psychoterapeuto, Łaskawy Czytelniku, Od Czterdziestu Dwóch Lat Już Wytężający Nadaremnie Słuch Sobowtórze." Stanisław Barańczak, "Wynosząc przed dom kubłz ze śmieciami" in *Widokówka z tego świata i inne rymy z lat 1986-1988* (Paris: Zeszyty Literackie, 1988).
8. Gorczyńska, 435.
9. Anna Czabanowska-Wróbel, "Ekonomia Liter" in *Obroty liter*, 316.
10. Anna Spólna, "Upiorne transformacje. Pytanie o moc słowa i kondycję poety w Literach Tomasza Różyckiego" in *Obroty liter*, 333-334.
11. Joseph Brodsky, "A Part of Speech" in *Collected Poems in English, 1972-1999* (New York: Farrar Straus and Giroux, 2000).

Acknowledgments

Thanks to the editors of the following journals in which these translations, some in different form, first appeared:

Asymptote: "Hair by Hair," "The Garden," "The Warmest Place," and "Sorting"

Atlanta Review: "Via Giulia," "At the End of the Day," and "This Era"

AzonaL: "To Give Water to the Thirsty," "First Poem for Menelik," "Twelve Letters," "White Dwarf," and "Pointers"

Cagibi: "Wind"

The Continental Literary Magazine: "What About Him?"

Copper Nickel: "Revenge Bank," "Two Days' Time," "Features," "Second Poem for Menelik," and "Open"

Guernica: "Phantom"

The High Window: "Summertime"

The Hudson Review: "A Glass"

Kenyon Review Online: "Third Planet"

Michigan Quarterly Review: "Scenario" and "Outside Prudnik"

New York Review of Books: "Clay" and "An Unexpected Turn of Events"

Northwest Review: "Mirror," "Euromaidan" and "Virus"

Plume: "A Room" and "Wild Strawberries"

Poetry: "Shadow"

Subtropics: "The Eternal War of Opposites," "Scent," and "Why"

Tupelo Quarterly: "No Answer" and "Essential Traits"

Two Lines: "Vacuum Theory," "Details," and "When Do Acacias Bloom?"

Zócalo Public Square: "Backpack"

The translator would like to express her gratitude to MacDowell, the Virginia Center for Creative Arts, the Anderson Center for Interdisciplinary Studies, Willapa Bay AiR, and the Polish Book Institute for invaluable time and space to complete the translation.

archipelago books
is a not-for-profit literary press devoted to
promoting cross-cultural exchange through innovative
classic and contemporary international literature
www.archipelagobooks.org